WITHDRAWN

29 REASONS

not to go to

LAW SCHOOL

BY RALPH WARNER, TONI IHARA & BARBARA KATE REPA

ILLUSTRATED BY MARI STEIN

NOLO PRESS BERKELEY

Printing History

Fourth Edition

Second Printing:	February 1996
Cover Design:	Toni Ihara
Illustrator:	Mari Stein
Proofreader:	Ely Newman
Printer:	Delta Lithograph

Warner, Ralph E.
  29 Reasons not to go to law school / by Ralph Warner & Toni Ihara. -- 4th national ed.
      p. cm.
  Includes index.
  ISBN 0-87337-243-3
  1. Law--vocational guidance--United States--Humor. 2. Law--Study and teaching--United States--Humor. 3. Law students--United States--Humor. 4. Practice of law--United States--Humor. I. Ihara, Toni Lynne. II. Title. III. Title: Twenty-nine reasons not to go to law school.
KF297.Z9W33 1994   94-350
340'.023'73--dc20   CIP

THANK YOU

The nicest thing about doing this book, except for the pleasure of working with each other, has been the good energy and support we have received from hundreds of former law students and lawyers. To say the least, most people still have intense feelings about the subject and it would have been easy to retitle this book "129 Reasons Not To Go To Law School." Particular thanks to all of those whose signed comments appear here. For several, contributing was an act of courage.

In addition, we would like to specially thank Anne Strick, Bob Keller, Michael Lowy, Craig Haney and F. Roy Willis. Their musings inspired many of the original reasons in the book.

And finally, a number of people made suggestions that were invaluable. Thanks to Jean Allen, Dan Armistead, Denis Clifford, Hayden Curry, Steve Elias, Patti Gima, Janice Kosel, Robin Leonard, Selma Mann, Carol Pladsen, Mary Randolph, Albin Renauer, Ray Reynolds, Eddie Warner and Andromache Warner.

Contents

FOREWARNING

The message you will read here subverts a cherished American folk fantasy—the one in which the sons and daughters of Pullman porters, shoe store clerks and cowboys go to the University, get awarded a Juris Doctorate degree and live happily ever after in the suburbs.

Our thesis is simple. Lawyering in the U.S., which has traditionally been one of the major crossroads where power and status merge to produce six-figure incomes, simply isn't what it used to be. These days, so many power-hungry young barristers are competing to pay the rent on their Porsches that getting a law license almost guarantees gridlock in a traffic jam of stalled careers.

And if one trouble with being a lawyer is that it just isn't the field it used to be, the main difficulty with law school is that it's exactly the institution it always was—still featuring the teaching methods of the Spanish Inquisition combined with a curriculum so enamored with the nineteenth century that it barely notices the twentieth and absolutely won't concede that a new one is fast approaching.

Since this book was first published in 1982, we have received dozens of letters from people who used it as part of the process leading up to their well-reasoned decisions not to go to law school.

We have also received a number of suggestions for additional reasons not to go to law school—most of them sent by lawyers. Many of these were so insightful that they have inspired us to add new material to the book. The result is that 29 Reasons has grown to 36 reasons.

Yes, yes—we know there are lots more. But we are determined that this little book not become as prolix, cumbersome and just plain heavy as the law books we warn you against.

LAW STUDENTS

reason 1. THE DRUDGE

Most law students don't want to get romantically involved with other law students. After studying law all day, who wants to talk it all night?

But during third year, a friend began dating a particularly intense classmate.

"How can you spend time with her?" I asked. "All she talks about is Contracts, Torts and Criminal Procedure."

"That's the idea," he said. "It's great practice for the bar exam."

RON OSTROFF
George Washington University National Law Center
Occupation: Business Writer

You can quickly identify this genderless type by the piquant but unmistakably musty odor it acquires the first week of fall semester when, for 102 consecutive hours, it barricades itself at the end of a library table behind a mountain of casebooks, hornbooks, annotated codes, federal reporters, legal encyclopedias, law dictionaries and law reviews.

While seeing The Drudge at work may initially make you smile, your good humor will last only until you realize that there are dozens of Drudges in your class that all spend 18 hours a day in the law library behind veritable Everests of legal material. That means that you will be competing with people who not only don't have a life, but don't want one.

As an additional vexation, when you need to do some research, you will never be able to find any assigned book on its proper shelf and will inevitably spend long hours going from library table to library table, exploring hundreds of Drudge hoards. For reasons that may have almost as much to do with its aversion to light and air as to its fear that a potentially needed bit of information will escape, no true Drudge ever reshelves a book.

The Drudge

At Work

At Leisure

On A Date

The Drudge's most inspiring characteristic is its iron constitution, exhibited by a number of bizarre behaviors.

1. It has the ability to go for days without sleep and three years without sex.

2. It has the skill to thrive without any exposure to natural light. Once a Drudge enters the physical plant of the law school, it lives much like the golem in its subterranean cavern, emerging pasty-faced and blinking on the day of The Bar Exam.

3. It has ox-like endurance, carrying pockets filled to bursting with the change needed to feed its closest companions—the law school machines. The Drudge has a particularly intimate relationship with the photocopier. It routinely stands for hours, reproducing every bit of recommended reading, every case cited in every footnote, every obscure minority opinion, and every word written by every professor in the law school, oblivious to the line of other students waiting to copy a page or two.

4. It has the talent to stare, ad infinitum, while the Lexis or Westlaw services drone out the latest subtle nuances to the latest arcane legal holding—as distinguished by the district court in

Pocatello, Idaho. While Drudges are normally mild, lethargic and slow to anger, they can turn instantaneously vicious if you come between them and their favorite terminal.

5. It has the constitution to exist exclusively on the cardboard donuts and tepid liquids available from the vending machines in the student lounge—reason enough for most people not to go to law school. Indeed, The Drudge appears to ingest the following with relish:

- a bitter, light brown caffeine-laced beverage that comes out of the same plastic tube as another liquid the vending company humorously refers to as Chicken Soup

- beef and bean burritos that stay cold in the center no matter how long they are left in the microwave, and

- ice cream drumsticks with leaky bottoms that taste like the glue used on the bindings of West's *Federal Reporters*.

reason 2. THE COMPULSIVE TALKER

The first day of school, I was abashed by the confident few who spouted legal lingo like erudite magpies. It took me a few weeks to see that they weren't generally the brighter students. Then I realized a sad thing: the vastly more sophisticated professors were only pretending to take these talkative students seriously. In fact, they were setting them up, maneuvering them closer and closer to the abyss of mid-term exams. When most of them crashed, they were never heard from again.

JERRY CARLIN
Yale Law School
Occupation: Painter

The Compulsive Talker

At Work

At Leisure

This is the law student who is the hardest to tolerate. Although Compulsive Talkers look pretty much like everyone else, once they enter a classroom, they are easy to spot.

Their right hands are usually waving frantically overhead in class. By the second year, their entire right arms are locked permanently in an overhead position.

Their voices are almost always loud, strident and shrill.

Although the content of their classroom remarks tends to oscillate between the painfully obvious, the painfully dumb and the painfully boorish, Compulsive Talkers are almost always exceedingly pleased with themselves.

They shout out wrong answers to rhetorical questions.

They lurk behind posts near lecture room doors before and after class—and in the stairwell near the library on weekends— from where they swoop down like crows from clotheslines to alternately interrogate and berate follow students. They specialize in bizarre questions on unread footnotes and love to hold forth on the brilliance and crucial importance of a dissenting opinion that they have first established their unsuspecting quarry do not

YOU'RE GOING TO LOVE THIS...
AND DON'T WORRY I'LL EXPLAIN
ALL THE IN-BITS... YOU KNOW..
FROM MY OWN PERSONAL
EXPERIENCE AND ALSO...

On a Date

know exist. Indeed, the Compulsive Talker depends on the fact that no normal student would ever read the piece of esoterica in question so that it can first feel superior and then fill you in ad nauseam. Your best way of dealing with Compulsive Talkers is not to respond. If you're lucky, the C.T.s you meet will be so busy carrying on a lively and even contentious dialogue with themselves that they won't notice when you slip away.

They do poorly on exams, to the surprise of no one but themselves.

They pass the Bar Exam on the second try and take jobs as assistant district attorneys in charge of prosecuting people who fail to pay their parking tickets.

reason 3. THE ASS KISSER

To keep from being bored to tears, the few fun-loving students in our class banded together to play the time-honored law school game: Asshole Bingo. We made slightly modified bingo cards with grids of the names of the classmates who were the most eager, most arrogant, most likely to raise their hands in class the most often. As the Know-It-Alls piped up to answer, we marked off their names. The first player to yell out "Bingo!" and produce a properly filled card got a free beer at Clyde's, the watering hole down the street.

Thomas Reynolds
Florida State University College of Law
Occupation: Art Dealer

Easy to pick out in any crowd, The Ass Kisser is the one cozying up to the one or two other people he or she thinks can lend the highest grade, the best position, the most prestige.

After the first few weeks of law school, The Ass Kisser will presume to speak of the teachers there in terms of endearment: My Civil Pro Professor, My Ethics Professor, My Maritime Law Professor. A.K.s invariably sit themselves next to the best briefwriter in class, from whose work they glibly quote when called upon in class.

After class, they can often be found perched in faculty offices—appearing to listen intently as the profs pronounce on about the pros and cons of pendent and concurrent jurisdiction.

This Apple For The Teacher selective coddling serves them well throughout their legal careers. In court, their tongues twist easily around the most elevated epithets: Judge, Your Honor, Your Most Immortal Holiness. And at the Big Firms, they effortlessly sacrifice their pride by feigning golf losses to senior partners blottoed by Sazeracs by the third hole.

The world's only hope for comeuppance: The Ass Kisser will be driven from office for soliciting graft shortly after being elected Senator.

YOUR MOST
IMMORTAL
HOLINESS...

reason 4. THE EAGER BEAVER

As an eager pre-law student, I enrolled in an undergraduate Environmental Law class in hopes of learning brilliant legal strategies to protect the environment. Our first classroom exercise was to compute how much Reynolds Aluminum had to pay in damages for killing people and then, to figure out if that was a cost-effective approach—that is, whether it made more sense to pay off the deceaseds' relatives and keep killing people than to remodel its plant to comply with pollution controls. I decided then not to go to law school.

Suzy Anderson
Occupation: Marketing Specialist, Legal Self-Help Publisher

Eager Beavers fixate on the lichens on the bark of each tree and miss the grander view of the forest. They approach each new law school lecture as a recording challenge—arriving equipped with tape recorder and video recorder, as well as the standard yellow pads, notebooks, pens, back-up pens and passel of color-coded highlighting pens.

When the day's classes are done, Eager Beavers quickly dart back to their lairs, which are invariably strewn with fast food wrappers and half-forgotten, half-eaten tacos and chicken wings. Once inside, they set to the task of transcribing and retranscribing the day's notes, tapes and films—all the while checking them against old class outlines purchased for $100 each from several different upperclassmen, all of whom claim to be editor of the law review.

Done in by the details, Eager Beavers have no time to study or to prepare for the next day's classes. Almost sadly, not one Eager Beaver makes it through first semester finals. The more severe cases are usually discovered months later, buried beneath mountains of obsolete study aids.

Less severe cases quit and become successful accountants.

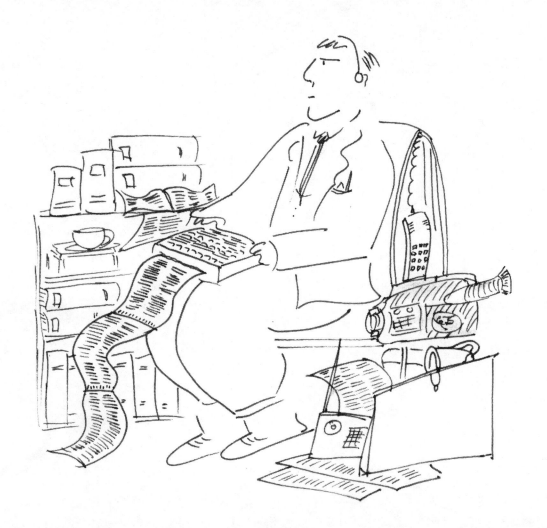

reason 5. THE INFORMATION STEALER

As each quarter drew to a close, fear of one's classmates gaining an unfair advantage mounted ominously. No one was exempt from suspicion. "See that blind man?" someone in the library would whisper. "I'll bet he is a first year student with 20/20 vision. He's probably escaping with the new Supreme Court abortion decision rolled into the hollow tip of his cane."

KATHY REIGSTAD
University of Washington School of Law
Occupation: Production Editor

Study syllabi in most law school courses are supplemented with Required Reading Lists, which mainly include voluminous, multi-footnoted law review articles with titles such as: "Late-Filed Chapter 22.1 §22(c) Petitions and the Doctrine of Judicial Scrutiny: Boon or Boondoggle?"

The treatises, written by the very professors who deem them essential, are obscure indeed, and can only be found in the Reserved Section in the bowels of the law school library.

Information Stealers relish such assignments. Unsheathing their single-edged razor blades, they deftly slice out the assigned pages, fold them into small squares so they fit easily into their plastic pocket protectors and hightail it home. There, they digest the verbiage. Often literally.

Information Stealers may have met their match in the Information Superhighway—nonspeak for a computerized store-and-retrieve method so desperate for information that it's willing to include obscure and meaningless treatises off its modems. It does not yield to razor blades.

As a consequence, many heartier Information Stealers have mutated to become proficient in Lexis/Nexis. They are the besuited ones hovering around the law library computers while the printers spit out reams of recent cases decisions and texts of pending legislation. If pressed, some will admit that they found employment as clerks at local law firms only after assuring the hiring partners that they could deliver free, unlimited access to online research.

reason 6. THE PARANOID

*First year, before exams, the fear was so heavy that you could
see it, taste it, even walk on it. When the first exam began, I
was the only one who was mellow. Of course, I always hold
my right wrist with my left hand to keep it from shaking.*

TED MASSEY
University of Minnesota Law School
Occupation: Advocate for Low Income People

Most Paranoids are ever-vigilant, their reflexes honed to a razor's edge. For example, one famous Harvard law Paranoid would, at the merest glance from a professor, jump out of his seat and do two somersaults while reciting seven alternative holdings for the case under discussion, concluding with: "I'm really not prepared, sir"—all before the professor had the chance to recheck the seating chart in an effort to call on the person two rows behind.

Unfortunately, Paranoids can be hard to spot. In an atmosphere where suspicion will invariably get you further than generosity, and where it rarely pays to dabble in Truth and Justice when you can score far more points by picking nits off another student's argument, all but a few law students qualify. One law professor has, however, developed what she considers to be a sure way to separate garden variety, competition-mad law students from real Paranoids. She calls it her Easy Test Ploy. It consists of giving an exam consisting of only simple and obvious questions. True Paranoids always flunk. Able to accept nothing at face value, they always assume that the straightforward and obvious can only be designed to mask hidden meaning. As a result, they fill their exam books with every answer save the right one. By contrast, average—mildly paranoid—students manage to pass, hanging on to a slender thread of common sense which

The Paranoid

At Work

At Leisure

On a Date

allows them to allude to the obvious answer before diluting and embroidering it with a myriad of alternative solutions. Sadly, the professor notes that those who do well on this exam tend not to make it through the first year.

Because believing in everything and nothing simultaneously requires such studious, albeit schizophrenic, attention to detail, some Paranoids eventually throw in their delusions and metamorphose into Drudges. (See Reason 1.) You can usually identify these hybrid creatures through their relationship to the coffee machine. They approach with Drudge-like determination, produce three quarters from bulging pockets, insert them resolutely and then jump back three paces in case the machine blows up like the one in *Flackey v. City of Tampa*, 620 U.S. 889.

reason 7. THE MONEY GRUBBER

The start of my law school career coincided with the start of the Reagan '80s, the decade when greed was hailed as a national hero. At a Dress For Success Seminar, the placement director told female students to strive for a look of Asexual Femininity when interviewing with the big law firms for high-paying jobs. When I saw my classmates earnestly taking notes, I knew I didn't belong there.

MARY RANDOLPH
University of California at Berkeley School of Law
Occupation: Editor

Many law students could care less about The Law. They go to law school for one reason: Money. From the moment they open their first Introduction to Evidence books, they talk incessantly of the $80,000 starting salaries they will pull down if they land a cubicle at one of the big name law factories in New York or Los Angeles. And, of course, that's only the beginning of a career that will quickly produce a seven-figure income and fill the six-car garage with Lamborghinis. A hot topic of debate is the merit of not practicing law at all, but going directly into Investment Banking—where they can get their hands on even more money: their own and their clients'.

The Money Grubber never seems to see beyond all those hypnotic zeros to realize that he or she must put in a ridiculous number of hours, including most weekends, to stay on the super success track. Even if The Money Grubber winds up with a personal jet, it will have been at the sacrifice of almost everything that makes life worth living. Another elusive realization is that many thousands of other Money Grubbers with exactly the same dream will be vying for a very few corner offices. It's not lonely enough on your way to the top.

The Money Grubber

You may be thinking: "Why should I care? I'm not a Money Grubber, and if others are, so be it."

Bear in mind that being trapped for three years with lots of people of such limited imagination would be a numbing experience.

Worst of all, greed can be contagious.

LAW SCHOOL

reason 8. THE BOREDUMB

One of my earliest law school experiences involved attending the finals of the school's Moot Court Competition. A big, white German Shepherd was lying across the aisle. About half-way through the competition, the dog began to yawn, and eventually fell asleep, snoring loudly. The dog was far more entertaining than the competition.

ROBIN LEONARD
Cornell Law School
Occupation: Editor

Perhaps the best reason to avoid the hallowed halls of schools of law: It's boring in there. Really boring.

If you spend too much time inside, you'll become boring, too.

reason 9. THE CLASSROOMS

Much of what went on in a law school lecture was like a bad melodrama. The professors, who awarded themselves the only starring role, were more interested in winning arguments and hogging center stage than in supplying information.

TONY MANCUSO
University of California Hastings College of Law
Occupation: Jazz Musician

Atmosphere: Ponderous and permeated with bloodlust. Even the most serene student feels like a Christian hors d'oeuvre about

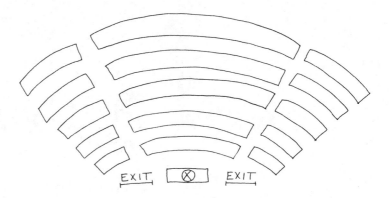

to be served up to the law professor lion. Grooves worn into the edge of the desks by the clutching fingers of generations of fearful students dreading their turns for public inquisition bear further witness to the quasi-religious roots of the law.

  Design: Ingeniously modeled along the lines of a Roman gladiatorial arena. Professors equipped with the dread instrument of torture known as The Seating Chart can easily single out

and nail their hapless victims to a cross of Contracts, Torts, or Criminal Procedure. As the floor plan illustrates, not only is there is nowhere to hide, escape is rendered impossible by the deliberate placement of the doors at the professor's back.

And the physical setting is only the beginning of a student's problems. Even more subversive is the style of the inquisition. Just as in Spain in the Middle Ages or in Stalin's Gulag, if you should miraculously manage to produce a right answer, it will never be sufficient. You will always be questioned further, through the use of ever more recondite hypotheticals, until you inevitably fail. For in this game of Socratic Madness, you are only allowed to play two roles—fall guy or straight man—depending on whether the professor casts himself or herself as prosecutor/persecutor or as the suave master of subtle nuance and gentle mockery. Either way, the result will be the same. The professor will have the last word. And you will feel used and foolish.

In fairness, some students derive considerable benefit from this firsthand training in the art of public humiliation. After all, they will spend their working lives in a profession where the ability to humiliate others is seen as a valuable skill.

reason 10. THE LAW PROFESSORS

The third week of law school, a surly Torts professor commonly known for his theatrical belittling of students became especially vexed at a student who seemed to have a somewhat loose grip on the concept of proximate cause. "Mr. Sullivan!" the professor thundered. "You are a worthless piece of humanity who shouldn't have bothered waking up today!" Sullivan took the command to heart, quit law school and became a residential real estate broker in Chicago. Two years later, his firm evicted the professor from his lakefront condo for nonpayment of rent.

ANONYMOUS
University of Chicago Law School
Occupation: Fitness Consultant

Most Law Professors were formerly Drudges (see Reason 1)—and after years of post-law school Drudgelike existences, have attempted to elevate pallid skins and questionable social skills to things to be revered. Objectively, this is difficult to swallow.

Also unpalatable is the fact that most Law Professors, those self-selected prophets sent down to train you in the practice of law, have never themselves practiced law, so are clueless about its actual whys and wherefores. To distract you from this realization, they will concentrate all of their flagging energy on Acting Law Professorlike, a fulltime job that involves:

- Squeezing themselves into faded tweed sports jackets with patched elbows (male model) or straight, mid-knee length scratchy wool skirts (female model) originally purchased decades ago for their first unsuccessful Big Firm interviews. Tobacco-filled pipes, for that look of heavy contemplation, are still de rigueur—although some opt to mouth the bows of their horn-rimmed glasses, instead.

THAT'S A CLOSE CONSTITUTIONAL QUESTION ... THE FOOTNOTES ON PAGES 972, 984, 999""

- Beginning the answer to every question with: "That's a close constitutional question"—followed by long-winded equivocations heavily padded with phrases such as "essentially," "moreover" and "Will there be an open bar?"

- Staking out an unclaimed corner of the law—to wit: jurisdictional ramifications of rhinoceros hunting—in which to become a Foremost Expert.

- Compiling wordy treatises on the topics in which they deem themselves Foremost Experts. All tenure decisions will be based on the number of footnotes included.

- Avoiding regular social interactions at all costs. Some law profs do let themselves out once a year—to attend the annual meeting of the American Association of Law Schools. At such gatherings, they can be spotted poolside, casually attired in bermudas and black socks and shoes. Sounds tough. No wonder they're surly.

reason 11. THE CASEBOOKS

Toward the middle of my first year, I had a rare moment of enlightenment. Timidly, I approached my favorite professor— the only one who didn't inspire fear in my heart. "It's just a thought," I began apologetically, "but is it possible that . . . well, it's crazy and I can't imagine why they would do it . . . but, it seems to me that some of these cases begin to make a little sense if you believe that the judge decided which way to rule first and then twisted the facts and the law to fit?" The good man laughed and put his arm around my shoulder. "Welcome to the law," he said.

DIANNA WAGGONER
New College of California School of Law
Occupation: Journalist

Physical Appearance: There are three principal colors: bruise blue, open wound red and bile green.

Size: Not one under five pounds. They are weighty in this sense, if in no other.

Guts: Deadly, double-columned rows of small tight type with even duller, smaller rows of footnotes guaranteed to make you squint until you scream. They are unrelieved by design, color, illustration or common sense.

Style: A rhetorical one best described as Baroque Legalese; literal corpulence; miles of print searching for a inch of meaning; inane repetition of the obscure; obtuse overkill in extremis.

The Intimate Albatross Factor: Law professors, who know more about guilt-inducing than the IRS and almost as much as your mother, insist that you have their leaden tomes in your possession at all times. You have full discretion in deciding whether you:

- clutch them to your bosom

- strap them to your back

• stuff them into a briefcase, satchel, bikebag or wheelbarrow,

or

• employ two sherpas and a yak.

Message: From grammar school through college, your books have always had a point to them—a fairly straightforward lesson to be learned. Math books teach you that 1 + 1 = 2. Spanish books teach you that uno, dos, tres = one, two, three. Anatomy books teach you that philogyny divided by ontogyny equals your appendix. Above all, the instruction process within these text-books is orderly. Juan y Maria learn to say "Buenos Dias" before they tackle windmills with Don Quixote.

When it comes to casebooks, however, the simple cannot be counted on to precede the complex. They are as full of the written reports of cases that reach the wrong result for the wrong reason as they are with those that reach the right result for the right reason. And then there are the nonsensical anomalies—decisions that have apparently been included only to demonstrate the absurdity of the judicial retirement system, which forces no judge to step down who can still find the way to the bathroom.

Yet despite their inherent nonsensicalness, legal casebooks in ever dizzying numbers have persisted, been duplicated and been the subjects of endless new editions. Among another reasons:

- They are the time-honored dinosaurs of a profession that only reluctantly substituted school for the apprenticeship method of reading random judicial decisions in the hope that they would eventually make sense.

- The essential nonsense of the casebook method pleasantly enhances the power of the law professor as the fount of all wisdom.

- Law professors don't have to read them. They rely instead on Teachers' Cheat Editions. These not only provide simple summaries of each case, but also contain numerous hypothetical questions—with answers—cleverly designed to torment even the most stubborn of students.

- Law professors ostensibly write them—acquiring more job security in their leaden careers each time their names are stamped across the spines of the bloated books. In fact, law professor authors do little more than collate collections of antiquated cases penned by judges. But they love to reap the royalties on the casebooks that invariably end up on their own Required Reading lists.

reason 12. WEEKENDS

If you go to school in the north, you struggle with climate. In winter, the weather can be so miserable that even a weekend spent with dead, dull law books is not so bad, as the library at least is warm. But it is otherwise when there is life and growth outside. When recalling sitting in the law library on beautiful spring Minnesota weekends, I can only think of the poem which says, "I have a rendezvous with death, when spring comes north this year. . . ."

MARLIN KASTAMA
University of Minnesota Law School
Occupation: Craftsperson

WE'LL BE ALONE AT LAST!

THE SKI WEEKEND: *Equipment List*

1 Torts casebook

2 legal pads

1 Contracts casebook

2 Gilbert's Outlines—Real Property and Criminal Law

3 class notebooks

1 bottle of No-Doz

1 bottle of eyedrops

3 pens

Helpful Hint: Long woolen underwear is helpful for studying past 2 a.m. and a colorful hat and scarf will get you into the spirit of the weekend. Don't bother with skis, however. You won't have time to use them.

THE SUPER BOWL WEEKEND: *Planning Ahead*

N.B.: All time allotments allow for vending machine and toilet usage.

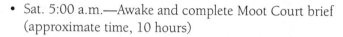

- Sat. 5:00 a.m.—Awake and complete Moot Court brief (approximate time, 10 hours)
- Sat. 3:00 p.m.—Go to law library, work on Contracts research paper(approximate time, 9 hours)
- Sun. 5:00 a.m.—Start reading and briefing cases for Monday's classes—Contracts, Civil Procedure and Remedies (approximate time, 8 1/2 hours)
- Sun. 2:00 p.m.—Sit down in front of television to enjoy game
- Sun 2:08 p.m.—Fall asleep just after kick-off
- Sun. 4:49 p.m.—Wake up as game ends and head for law library

Helpful Hint: Resolve not to waste so much time next weekend.

THE LOST WEEKEND: *Equipment List*

With a former lover who turns up and won't take "Sorry, I'm behind in Crim Law" for an answer.

1 cassette tape, *The Joy of Guilt*

1 self-help book, *Up from Celibacy: A Guidebook for Lapsed Monks and Others Who Have Forgotten How or Never Knew*

1 reference book, *The Non-Lawyer's Guide to Common Legal Slang*—for your friend

Helpful Hint: You need not bother with birth control devices. Your attempt at total withdrawal from manic study will almost surely be too anxiety-producing to allow for their use. Be prepared for your self-control to snap within an hour of arriving at the romantic cabin. It is a perfectly normal reaction to fondle the Real Property outline hidden within the folds of that teddy, and desperately seize upon the Criminal Procedure book you buried in the picnic basket. To regain equilibrium, lock yourself in the equipment closet with your books, shut your eyes and pretend you never left the law library.

reason 13. BAD BACKS, BAD EYES, GENERAL SICKLINESS

For three years, the stacks of law books I lugged about gave me a chronic backache, as well as eye strain and a generally depressed outlook on the world. When I graduated from law school and became a fisherman, I almost tossed them out. That would have been a terrible mistake. Prosser on Torts, Black's Law Dictionary and the rest of the collection have finally become extremely useful tools. I use them to press smoked salmon into lox.

RICHARD BELL
University of California Hastings College of Law
Occupation: Salmon Fisherman

During your three years of pre-Esquire servitude, you are almost guaranteed to develop one or all of the following physical deformities: Bad Eyes, a Bad Back and General Sickliness.

Bad Eyes: The cause of this condition is pretty CLEAR—unless you're a law student who has not yet seen an optometrist, in which case you will be squinting. Each year, law students read the equivalent, both in volume and interest, of six Manhattan phone books and the collected works of Danielle Steele. This incipient blindness, accompanied by chronic confusion, most often produces a fairly noticeable wrinkling of the brow. This can be turned into a considerable asset later on, as clients often mistake it for a look of intense professional concern.

Bad Back: Not as severe as Quasimodo's condition, but a definite curvature of the spine occurs after three years of relentless toting around and hunching over *Prosser on Torts*, *Williston on Contracts* and *Louisell on Pleading*. Some students try to avoid this condition by studying while seated in backless, Ergonomically Correct chairs. This group can be easily identified by their bowed-backward knees.

General Sickliness: Nowhere breathes a weaker-constitutioned, more out of shape, more pallid group than in a law school classroom. Most within their walls suffer from non-specific symptoms of exhaustion, mild nausea and poor circulation. When consulted, doctors normally shrug and smile maliciously—having felt even worse throughout med school. Sufferers—and that includes almost all law students, with the possible exceptions of The Drudge, The Compulsive Talker and The Ass Kisser (see Reasons 1, 2 and 3)—want to go to bed and pull the covers over their heads for three years. Of those who do, 100% have reportedly been cured. The great suffering majority, however, swig from bottles of Maalox and plug along, saving their bile for that savorous day when they file their first medical malpractice action.

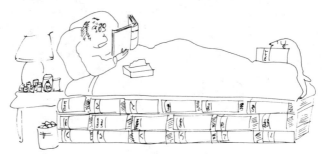

reason 14. LEARNING TO BE LAWYERLY

Law school violates not only your basic constitutional right of freedom of speech, but your even more precious personal right to think for yourself. You may try to resist for a while, but unless you are truly mad in the best sense of that word, law school will eventually mold you into one of its clones.

ELAINE KOWALL
University of California at Berkeley School of Law
Occupation: Program Director, Special Education

THE FIRST DAY OF LAW SCHOOL

A middle-aged professor stands before a roomful of bright, confident, articulate students. All have worked hard and achieved top grades for years. They are in a good mood, plainly delighted by what they regard as a new challenge. In contrast, the professor seems washed out and haggard. Several students wonder if he is up to the job ahead.

THE 10TH DAY OF LAW SCHOOL

The professor has assigned and discussed a few hundred cases. They are presented out of context and out of order. An 1840 decision from a Massachusetts court follows one decided in Los Angeles in 1967, which comes after a 14th century English opinion. When a particular decision appears to make internal sense, students gratefully grasp at it as they might a life raft on a stormy sea. Unfortunately, their slender hold on security is soon washed away by the next wave of cases, which arrive at completely different conclusions.

The cases do, however, have one thing in common: they all introduce new jargon and unfamiliar concepts which are nowhere defined. Students, mostly former Political Science majors, desperately try to fathom the basic ethical and moral principles on which the new material rests. The professor airily dismisses these attempts not merely as wrong or unworkable, but with the most damning indictment of all: No one is thinking like a lawyer.

INTERIM RESULT

Confusion and disorientation are rampant. Most students conclude that the only way to get through the material is to dig harder and faster. Others become depressed and think of quitting. A few do quit, breathing great sighs of relief. The majority, who have elected to stay, pretend not to notice.

THE 20TH DAY

The professor has become more demanding. Students who persist in trying to see legal information in the context of a larger world view are routinely humiliated. Those who look no further than what Justice Marshall opined in *Marbury v. Madison* and refer confidently to the Rule in *Shelley's Case* are praised. As a result, fewer students persevere in involving considerations of good, bad, right or wrong. More students resolve to try to think like lawyers.

INTERIM RESULT

Gone are the days when the students seemed interested and interesting. When several more students drop out, they are jeered as abject failures by those who remain.

THE 30TH DAY

The professor is relaxed now, almost friendly. Any hope students may have held of relating their law school experience to the larger picture has given way to a feverish determination to master the technicalities of their new field. They now pride themselves in the use of legal lingo, compete in trying to remember the names of esoteric cases mentioned in casebook footnotes and answer hypothetical questions by referring only to well-established legal precedent. Even when they get *res ipsa loquitur* mixed up with *res judicata*, the professor benignly encourages them. Now that they are all members of the same club, it seems

BUT I CAN'T ARGUE THAT SIDE
OF THE CASE — IT'S NOT RIGHT.
I CAN'T TAKE THE SIDE OF
IMPRISONMENT AND TORTURE.

HMM — HERE'S JUSTIFICATION
FOR DETAINING THEM IN
REFUGEE CAMPS. THERE IS
NO "INTERNATIONAL RIGHT
OF ASYLUM." WE HAVE NO
LEGAL RESPONSIBILITY FOR
STATELESS PEOPLES.

LOCK 'EM UP
AND THROW AWAY
THE KEY!

to matter little if it takes some longer to learn to properly knot their professional obfuscations than it does others.

FINAL RESULT

The students have come full circle. Their confusion and helplessness have given way to a swaggering feeling of power and exhilaration. They are back on top. They have given up trying to understand how law can help regulate a decent society or worrying about how to resolve disputes justly.

They have learned to think like lawyers.

reason 15. KISSING LOVE GOODBYE

At a cocktail party during my second year I overheard the following conversation between two young women:

"What form of birth control do you use?"

"Oh, I don't use any—my husband is a law student."

> JEANNE S. STOTT
> University of San Francisco School of Law
> Occupation: Small Claims Advisor

FREQUENCY OF SEXUAL ENCOUNTERS

NB: *If married to or living with another law student, frequency rates should be halved.*

SEXUAL FREQUENCY IF MARRIED OR LIVING WITH SOMEONE:

Before Law School	*During Law School*
Three times per day	Once a week
Once a day	Once a month
Four times a week	New Year's Eve
Once a week	Don't hold your breath

SEXUAL FREQUENCY IF SINGLE

Before Law School	*During Law School*
Once a day	Once a semester
Four times a week or less	Try masturbation

reason 16. MORTGAGING THE FUTURE

I entered law school so I could get an interesting job and make enough money to afford an $800 Martin guitar. I spent over $16,000 on three-piece suits, law books, and law school loans. Then I discovered that practicing law and having an interesting job is a contradiction in terms. The few jobs available that did sound like fun paid almost nothing. Now I'm $8,000 in debt and I still can't afford the guitar.

ALBIN RENAUER
University of Michigan Law School
Occupation: Software Development Coordinator

The cost of law school keeps rising. Three years at Stanford cost $66,000. Northwestern is a bargain at a mere $54,000. And that's just tuition. Rent, food, books and three-piece interview suits are necessary extras that can easily double these numbers. Of course, students on ADC (All Daddy's Cash) can afford such expenses without batting an eye. But for the average American recent college grad trying to make it at least somewhat independently, these are big numbers indeed.

And so Financial Aid beckons to many. It's easy. It's quick. And it feels good while you're doing it. In fact, there are no problems with it—until they cut you off. As with many other addictions, it's the hangover that's the killer. It's not uncommon for graduates of private law schools to leave with debts of over $50,000, plus interest. People entering school now can figure on paying off law school with healthy monthly payments from the day they graduate until the year 2010.

This, too, is not a problem for those who work 80 hours a week and charge their clients $225 per hour. But if you want to use your legal skills to help people, and to charge fees ordinary people can afford, you will have to get used to the idea of being heavily in debt until the third quarter of 2040.

reason 17. READING LATRINALIA

Someone ran a contest on the wall of a toilet wall in the Women's Restroom as to which law professor you would like to spend a weekend with on a deserted island.

The winner: a vibrator, hands down.

ANONYMOUS
University of Alabama School of Law
Occupation: G.O. at Club Med

In Graffiti Veritas...

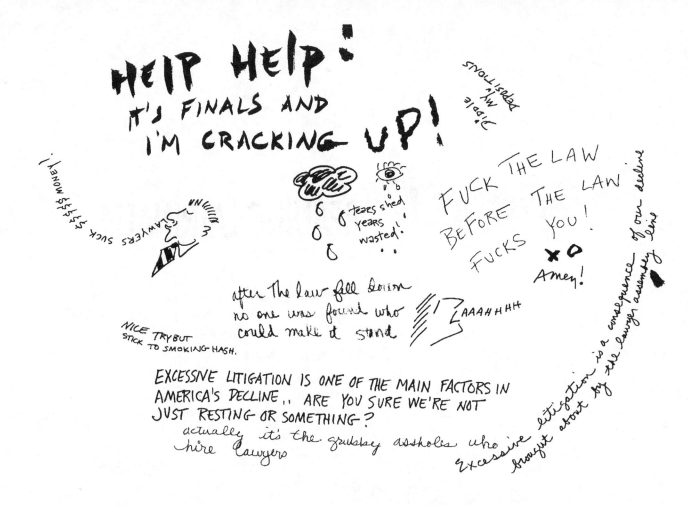

Copied Off The Restroom Walls in Boalt Hall School of Law,

KISS FREEDOM GOODBYE!

Kiss my briefs! smack!

anyone who enters this building will die of boredom.

—YAWN!

THE WORLD HATES LAWYERS,
TO TOP IT OFF, YOU CAN'T EVEN GET
A JOB WHEN YOU GRADUATE. CONCLUSION:
QUIT THIS PLACE AND GO TO THE BEACH —

Lawyers teach
corruption to
the unwary.

WHAT SEX LIFE?

STATISTICS ARE LIKE
LAWYERS.... THEY CAN
NEVER B TRUSTED

DOCTORS TAKE THE HIPPOCRATIC OATH
LAWYERS TAKE THE OATH OF HYPOCRISY!

YOU FAIL TO CONSIDER THAT
STATISTICS SAY THAT
LAWYERS ARE LIARS
SO THEY CAN'T BE LIARS

University of California

reason 18. THE BAR EXAM

It was the second day of the bar exam. On my way up the hill to the examination room that sunny morning, I realized that I'd rather be writing children's stories.

PETER JAN HONIGSBERG
New York University School of Law
Occupation: Author, children's folk tales

Imagine spending three years:

- memorizing the contents of 26 feet, 7 inches of books (approximately 911 pounds, for those readers who are heavy thinkers)

- listening to 1,800 hours of lectures

- taking 30 examinations, and

- going through $80,000 to $150,000.

Then imagine being told that all your reading, all your listening, all your success on the examinations and all your money qualify you for absolutely nothing except the right to take one more test: The Bar Examination.

Imagine being told that The Bar Exam tests not so much what you learned in the 1,800 lecture hours or the 26 feet, 7 inches of books, but on your ability to completely memorize the contents of an 8-inch thick outline.

Imagine next being told that to get this outline, you must pay an additional $1,700 and spend a couple of months at another school: The School of Bar Review.

Imagine going to this new school with the knowledge that even if you read the magic outline 18 hours a day, evict your dog and sleep with the bar outline clutched to your breast, your chances of flunking the examination are one in two.

Imagine sitting in The Bar Examination for three days, surrounded by gray-faced classmates trying desperately to make it into the top 50%.

Imagine how you will feel if you succeed.

Imagine how you will feel if you fail.

Imagine how you will feel if you do something entirely different with your life.

Imagine how you will feel if you succeed   Imagine how you will feel if you fail

BECOMING A LAWYER

reason 19. TALKING LIKE A LAWYER

One day in Property class, we were on the topic of covenants and had just finished discussing whether they were executed or executory, express or implied, general or specific, principal or auxiliary, joint or several, inherent or collateral or just plain disjunctive, when the professor nailed this poor guy at the back of the class. He cleared his throat and asked, "Mr. Wason, tell us about the springing uses of covenants that run with the land."

That was the last straw for Wason. He jumped from his seat, spilled his books onto the floor and then, looking like a crazed space cadet, started babbling about "springing, jumping,

leaping, bounding, twirling, flying uses..." When he finally
wound down, he just ran out of the classroom.

PHAEDRA B. DADRA
University of Santa Clara School of Law
Occupation: Food Consultant

You—with your A+ term papers and secret poems hidden under your shiny new bachelor's degree. You probably think that you are a competent, perhaps even facile, speaker of the Queen's English. In fact, it may well be your ability to make words do backflips in mid-sentence that leads you to contemplate a career in a profession which uses them as both spear and shield.

Before you sign up for the LSAT, though, take a closer look at the official language spoken by the Lords and Ladies of the Court of Law.

Listen for a minute to the Great Goddess Gobbledygook.

You say you can't understand a thing she is saying, but she seems to be saying whatever she is saying at least twice and often thrice and quite impressive it all sounds, too? You have a quick and intuitive ear. Without a doubt you have the knack to pick up legal language in record time.

The Great Goddess Gobbledygook and Her Subjects

YE OLDE FAVORITE LEGALISMS

Pray the Court: Archaic English

Voir Dire: Obsolete French

Oyer, trouver: Archaic English descended from Obsolete French

Peturbatrix (a woman who breaks the law): Whimsical

Certiorari: Middle English from Latin

Mens rea, pendente lite, res adjudicata, assumpsit: Latin

Gebocced: Anglo-Saxon

Garathinx: Old Lombardic

Hereditaments: Sicilian and Neapolitan

Fee simple, equitable title, proximate cause, insanity: Familiar words that have special legal meanings

You say these seem to be no more than bits of jargon and not a language at all. Right you are again.

Legalese is not a language on the order of French or Spanish or even Pig Latin—all of which share a logical structure and internal coherence. With these languages, once the rules are learned, comprehension is close behind. Not so with the language of the law. Each term or phrase is its own arbitrary, mind-boggling mystery—vowels and consonants dragged from the scrap heap of history, bearing no logical relationship to one another and conveying no meaning that could not be put more easily in Plain English.

But surely, you say, there must be some reason for using all this jargon to obfuscate what seems to be simple enough concepts. Of course there is, and it goes far beyond the words themselves—straight to the core of the profession: *acquisitive circumlocutio in gross.*—The Longer the Words, the Higher the Fee.

reason 20. THINKING LIKE A LAWYER

Soon after I entered law school, I realized that, just like the indoctrination aims of other cults, law school systematically brainwashes its converts. I was deprived of sleep (monstrous study loads), humiliated in public (sarcastic cross-examination by the instructor), told I would learn to think in a new way (like a lawyer) and promised salvation (lawyer status) if I would just stick it out. Unfortunately, there are few deprogrammers for this cult. I joined up for twelve years before circumstances—or fate—taught me that I'm not what I do. When I was finally able to stop practicing law, I began to rediscover my humanity.

STEVE ELIAS
University of California, Hastings College of Law
Occupation: Teacher and Writer

On Seeing an Auto Accident

CAN I HELP?

IS THERE PROXIMATE CAUSE?

HERE'S MY CARD.

Before Law School

Mid Law School

After Law School

On Seeing a Former Lover

YOU LOOK GREAT, LET'S GET TOGETHER LATER.

OH HI—NO I'M TOO BUSY FOR COFFEE.

I'LL DROP BY JUST AS SOON AS YOU SIGN THIS LITTLE PAPER THAT SAYS WE'RE JUST FRIENDS, MY INCOME IS MINE, YOU HAVE NO CLAIM TO...

Before Law School

Mid Law School

After Law School

On Seeing a Married Couple Quarreling

Before Law School

Mid Law School

After Law School

On Seeing A Slippery Spot on a Supermarket Floor

Before Law School

Mid Law School

After Law School

reason 21. LOOKING LAWYERESQUE

It was just so tedious dressing every morning as if I was going to my own funeral.

ANONYMOUS
Valparaiso University School of Law
Occupation: Between Careers

Question: Suppose you wanted 300 ordinary men and women—some vegetarian, some black, some brown, some tall, some in wheelchairs, some wearing T-shirts and sneakers, some riding motorcycles, some who secretly aspire to be rock stars, artists or poets—to dress in nondescript blazers, starched button down shirts and sensible black shoes, to wear glasses, to speak authoritatively in a strange and multi-syllabic language, to strut about determinedly with one shoulder hunched far lower than the other pulled by the weight of an ever-present hand-tooled Italian briefcase, to constantly check the watch on the other arm, grind their teeth, to interrupt whenever anyone begins to speak and to carry business cards in little gold engraved cases to the ski slopes?

Answer: Let them into law school. Keep them there three years. Let them out.

PASTE YOUR PICTURE
IN CIRCLE "A"

PASTE YOUR PICTURE
IN CIRCLE "B"

A

B

ADHERE TO
PICTURE IN
SECOND YEAR

ATTACH TO PICTURE
DURING FINALS
(CAUTION- DO NOT
REMOVE FROM THIS
TIME FORWARD.)

CUT ALONG
DOTTED LINE
(INSERT HAND
PERMANENTLY)

D. O. P.

CUT ALONG DOTTED LINE
(INSERT HAND UNTIL
CRAMP IS NO LONGER
FELT)

G.G.

ATTACH TO
ARM / BACK
AND/OR
ANYWHERE

WARNING: DANGER OF
PARANOIA ATTACK IF
REMOVED.

ATTACH FIRMLY
TO SHOULDER
(LEAVE IN PLACE
UNTIL SHOULDER
CONFORMS TO
SHAPE)

FREQUENT FURTIVE
GLANCES REQUIRED
THROUGHOUT DAY
AND NIGHT. DO NOT
REMOVE FROM WRIST
UNDER ANY CIRCUMSTANCES.

WEAR AT ALL TIMES
AND REFER TO EVERY
10 MINUTES.

reason 22. LIVING WITH OTHER LAWYERS

I heard a news item involving a claim of racial discrimination, but couldn't remember the precise constitutional test applied. I asked my lover—also an ex-lawyer—who couldn't recall either. Annoyed that our investment in law school tuition seemed to have been wasted, we spent the evening looking through our combined six years of law school notes. We eventually found the answer, but I can't help thinking that there must have been a better way to spend an evening.

LEE RYAN
Yale Law School
Occupation: Librarian

Lawyers often pair off to live together or marry. There are two reasons for this:

1. Other lawyers don't ask for free legal advice, and

2. Non-lawyers generally avoid lawyers on social occasions because they are contentious, boring and never offer to pay.

Witness newlyweds Barry (University of Tennessee School of Law '88) and Laverne (Cornell University School of Law '91) as they attempt to put aside their professional personas to enjoy a tranquil breakfast.

Barry: This is tasty french toast, dear. But didn't we agree to have raisin toast on weekends instead of wheat?

Laverne: Oh, honey, I think your memory of our agreement is erroneous. We decided to have raisin toast on the weekend morning that we didn't have french toast. As everyone knows, you can't make french toast with raisin bread.

Barry: I don't see why that presumption can't be rebutted, and anyway, we unequivocally agreed on weekends with raisin toast. In fact, I've been relying on it all week. I might even say that I've suffered genuine and irreparable pain and . . .

Laverne: No need to get adversarial, my dear. Now, I'm sure we can work out a sensible compromise.

Barry: Well, how about having raisin toast very Sunday morning except that on the mornings we have french toast, you can pick the raisins out of your pieces?

Laverne: You call that a compromise? I would urge you to consider instead that . . .

reason 23. GETTING NO RESPECT

Lawyers are upset. They have discovered what they believe to be an alarming new trend: People don't like them. The American Bar Association recently appointed a special panel to investigate the legal profession's bad image. The California State Bar commissioned a survey to find out why so many people hate lawyers. Legal conventions now regularly include sessions on the public's negative perception of lawyers.

We wish to reassure lawyers. This wave of anti-lawyer feeling is nothing new. People have always hated you.

> ANDREW AND JONATHAN ROTH
> Brothers of a lawyer
> Occupation: Legal Historians

I, Lucius Titus, have written this, my testament, without any lawyer, following my own natural reason rather than excessive and miserable diligence.

> The Will of a Citizen of Rome

It's better to enter the mouth of a tiger than a court of law.

> Ancient Chinese Proverb

St. Yves is from Brittany
A lawyer but not a thief
Such a thing is beyond belief

> A popular rhyme about a 14th century lawyer who was made a saint because he represented the poor

They have no lawyers among them for they consider them as a sort of people whose profession it is to disguise matters.

> Sir Thomas More, *Utopia* (1516), Of Law & Magistrates

That one hundred and fifty lawyers should do business together ought not to be expected.

Thomas Jefferson, from his autobiography
(on the U.S. Congress)

Always remember that when you go into an attorney's office door, you will have to pay for it, first or last.

Anthony Trollope, *The Last Chronicle of Barset*

I think we may class the lawyer in the natural history of monsters.

John Keats

Four sheep, a hog and ten bushels of wheat settled an Iowa breach of promise suit where $25,000 damages were demanded. The lawyers got all but the hog, which died before they could drive it away.

Item appearing in the *Cheyenne Leader,* January 14, 1888

Litigation is a machine which you go into as a pig and come out as a sausage.

Ambrose Bierce

Lawyers earn a living by the sweat of browbeating others.

James Gibbons Haneker

Lawyers: persons who write a 10,000 word document and call it a brief.

Franz Kafka

May your life be full of lawyers.

Mexican curse

For a good time, hire a hooker,
For a lot of time, hire my attorney.

Anonymous, Prison cell graffiti

I wouldn't write a song about any of them.

John Lennon

reason 24. SPEAKING IN TONGUES

The use of language in law can be described as Zen and the Art of Getting to the Point in the Most Excruciatingly Plodding Manner Possible. Rumor has it that style points are accumulated on this basis in law school. To the extent lawyers support the use of oppressive, circuitous, redundant and ponderous legalese, we are the authors of our own distress. I gained a lot of words in law school, but lost a language: English.

CHERYL A. ORVIS
George Washington University National Law Center
Occupation: Self-Employed Businessperson

NOW I LAY ME DOWN TO SLEEP
I PRAY THE LORD MY SOUL TO KEEP
IF I SHOULD DIE BEFORE I WAKE
I PRAY THE LORD MY SOUL TO TAKE.

AMEN.

BEDTIME PRAYERS BEFORE MOMMY WENT TO LAW SCHOOL

AT THE PRESENT JUNCTURE, THIS DAY AND AGE, THIS HOUR, ON THIS, THE PRESENT OCCASION; I, MYSELF, THIS PARTICULAR INDIVIDUAL AND ENTITY, ALLEGED TO BE MARY JOYCE HARCOURT AND SOMETIMES REFERRED TO AS "JOYCIE," OR "MUFFIN" (SOLE OFFSPRING OF HARLAN AND AMANDA HARCOURT); REPOSIT, ASSIGN AND CONSIGN, FIX AND ESTABLISH THIS SAID PERSON, THE ABOVE AND AFOREMENTIONED (SEE PARAGRAPH 1. LINE 3 AND 4. WORDS 26, 27, 29, 34 AND 36) WHO SHALL BE REFERRED TO AS THE PARTY OF THE FIRST PART FROM THIS TIME FORWARD, IN A LOWERED (AS COMPARED TO UPRIGHT) RECLINED AND/OR PROSTRATED POSITION, FOR THE SOLE PURPOSE OF SLUMBER, REPOSE, REST IN THE ARMS OF MORPHEUS, SOUNDLY AND/OR HEAVILY, LIKENED TO A TOP AND/OR LOG, NOT TO THE EXCLUSION OF DREAMING AND/OR SNORING WHICH SHALL REMAIN TO BE SEEN ON THE EVIDENCE OF THOSE WHO SHALL REMAIN ANONYMOUS AT THIS TIME; I, MYSELF, THIS PERSON, THIS PARTICULAR INDIVIDUAL AFOREMENTIONED AND NOW REFERRED TO AS THE PARTY OF THE FIRST PART PROPOSE, REQUEST AND PETITION, MAKE BOLD TO ASK, PUT TO AND CALL UPON, COURT, SEEK TO ENTREAT, AND IMPLORE, BESIEGE, IMPORTUNE AND ADJURE, BEG AND BESEECH THE DIVINE DEITY, GODSHIP, GODHEAD, OMNIPOTENT AND OMNISCIENT SPIRIT i.e. SUPREME BEING, SOUL, HIGHER POWER, PROVIDENCE, KING OF KINGS, QUEEN OF QUEENS, LORD OF LORDS, ALMIGHTY ONE, ABSOLUTE BEING, INFINITE CAUSE, SOURCE, UNIVERSAL MIND, NATURE, ALL POWERFUL, ETERNAL BEING, ALL KNOWING, ALL WISE, ALL MERCIFUL, ALL HOLY, THE PRESERVER, MAKER, CREATOR, AUTHOR, AND/OR CREATOR OF ALL THINGS, TRUTH AND LOVE AND BUNNIES; MY, THE AFOREMENTIONED PARTY OF THE FIRST PART, ESSENCE, FUNDAMENTAL TRUE BEING, INMOST NATURE, CORE, INNER AND ESOTERIC REALITY, VITAL CENTER, ESSENTIAL SELF AND SUCHNESS, QUIDDITY, PITH, KERNEL, NUCLEUS, INMOST RECESSES OF THE HEART, SPIRIT, PRANA, LIFE FORCE AND ELEPHANTS; TO TAKE CUSTODY OF, GUARD, WATCH OVER, SUSTAIN AND PRESERVE FOR THE SAFE KEEPING OF, AUSPICIOUS AND SECURE AND CAUTIOUS SURVELLANCE OF, TO PROTECT, HOLD AND KEEP. SHOULD CIRCUMSTANCES WARRANT THAT I, THE AFOREMENTIONED ONE, NOW KNOWN AS THE PARTY OF THE FIRST PART, SHOULD EXPIRE, END, CEASE TO LIVE, EXTINGUISH THE MORTAL LIGHT, LEAVE THIS PHYICAL PLANE, EXPERIENCE MY DEMISE, DESIST, QUIT THIS WORLD, MAKE MY EXIT, PASS ON, PASS AWAY, MEET MY END, SHUFFLE OFF THIS MORTAL COIL, RELINQUISH OR SURRENDER MY LIFE, YIELD THE GHOST, GIVE UP MY BREATH, GO OUT LIKE THE SNUFF OF A CANDLE, FORSAKE ALL BORDER COLLIES, BEFORE OR AT A TIME PRIOR TO THE TIME I REGAIN CONSCIOUSNESS, PASS FROM THE SLEEPING TO THE WAKING STATE, ROUSE MYSELF, WARM TO THE DAY, OPEN MY EYES, I, THE PARTY OF THE FIRST PART, IMPLORE, BEG AND BESEECH, INVOKE AND ENTREAT, HUMBLY ASK THEE ALMIGHTY, EVER PRESENT UNIFYER OF ALL PERSONS, PLACES AND THINGS, MAMMALS, FISH, BIRDS AND INSECTS, GIVER OF BOONS, ENERGY IN ALL FORMS, INSTILLER OF FAITH, HEALING SOURCE, ONE WHO GIVES ENDLESS LOVE UNCONDITIONALLY, MY, AS IN ME AND MINE, AS IN I, THE PARTY OF THE FIRST PART, OF MORTAL NATURE, SPIRIT, ATMA, BUDDHI, VITAL FORCE, INNER PRINCIPLE, HEART, MIND AND EMBODIED BREATH, ANIMATING PRINCIPLE AND TRUE SELF, INCLUDING TOADS WHO CALL THEMSELVES FIGARO, ESSENCE AND SUBSTANCE OF LIFE, THE DIVINITY THAT STIRS WITHIN, INNER FLAME AND SEAT OF CONSCIOUSNESS TO; (IF IT PLEASES THEE) APPROPRIATE, CAPTURE, SEIZE, ABDUCT WITH AND ACQUIRE FOR AN INFINITE PERIOD OF TIME, ENTER INTO POSSESSION OF, AND TAKE RESPONSIBILITY FOR, OBTAIN AND RESCUE, PICK UP, GLEAN, GATHER IN, CAPTURE AND SEIZE AND HOLD UNTIL SUCH TIME AS IT SHALL BE RELINQUISHED BY THE SAID HOLDER. AMEN.

Bedtime prayers after Mommy went to law schoool

reason 25. LIFE IMITATING COMPLICATIONS

How times have changed since the Republic was founded. Tell a lawyer today that you've just worked out a scheme that will establish justice, promote domestic tranquillity and ensure the general welfare, and he'll end up persuading you that if you're lucky and carefully follow his advice, you may end up not going to jail.

ROBERT KELLER
Columbia University School of Law
Occupation: Novelist

Somebody eventually has to gently tell a child that Santa Claus, the Easter Bunny and the Tooth Fairy don't exist. And it can be a real service if someone pricks the bubble of an unrealistic commercial or investment venture before it falls on its expensive face. Assuredly, there is a valuable role for a person who convincingly debunks all sorts of doubtful dreams and undertakings. Finding flaws is a skill that our society needs to have done well. But you should think and think again about whether you are ready and willing to assume a career that is professionally committed to finding flaws.

Suppose, for example, you do become a lawyer and two friends of yours, Sara and Jim, stop by to help you celebrate hanging out your first shingle. With stars in their eyes and beatific expressions on their faces, they tell you that they, too, have some wonderful news: they've decided to move in together. About two seconds after you propose a toast to Love Everlasting, a loose corner of your lawyer's brain sends up an alarm that causes you to furrow your brow, stroke your chin and casually mention the disturbing recent increase in palimony cases.

When Sara asks how celebrities fighting over millions of dollars affects the two of them, you explain that the legal decisions have established a precedent that boils down to the fact that to be legally safe, unmarried couples must reduce their understandings to writing.

You urge them to:

- inventory their separate possessions

- draw up an anticipatory property settlement agreement which delineates clearly whether income is to be shared equally or held separately if they split up

- design an agreement to cover James moving into Sara's house, which will also contain a schedule allowing his monthly payments to be turned into a share of the equity over time, and

- begin drafting a parenthood agreement, to cover contingencies that may arise if and when they have a child.

You are just warming to your task of contributing common sense to their star-struck venture when Sara notes: "Oops, we are running late and have to scurry."

Before

After

A few days later, Jim calls to thank you. It seems that until he and Sara talked to you, they simply did not understand all the possible legal downsides and worries that would come with moving in together. Jim then reiterates how grateful both he and Sara are for all of your advice. Finally, he promises that they will have you over for supper real soon.

They never do.

reason 26. THEY'RE ALL GONNA LAUGH AT YOU

I quit law after practicing for eleven years. My conclusion: If you want to find the law, go to law school. If you want to find justice, go to Small Claims Court.

PAUL ROSENTHAL
University of California Hastings College of Law
Occupation: Restaurant Owner and Chef

When people feel picked upon by a more powerful bully, they usually get angry. And eventually, many try to get even. One way to do this is to attack, using stealth or trickery. Another common approach is to subject the oppressive person or group to ridicule. The mean jokes that privates tell about their intimidating sergeants during wartime are one good example of this phenomenon. Another is Lawyer Jokes.

Face it. Everyday in every workplace, cafe and talk show in America, people delight in telling Lawyer Jokes for an excruciatingly simple reason. They hate how lawyers have twisted the American legal system into a professional piñata full of goodies for the legal profession and broken cardboard for everyone else.

And the sad thing is, even if you do your best to be a decent lawyer, your profession's miserable reputation will thwart your efforts to be seen as a caring person. Daily, your ears will be filled instead with barbs and ruins in the form of Lawyer Jokes which may include the sampling noted here.

Q: What's the difference between a terrorist and a lawyer?
A: The terrorist has supporters.

Q: *How many lawyers does it take to change a light bulb?*
A: Your bulb or theirs?

Q: *What do you get when you cross the Godfather with a lawyer?*
A: An offer you can't understand.

Q: *Why is an avocado like a lawyer?*
A: Both have hearts like stones.

Q: *What do you call a lawyer with an IQ of 40?*
A: Your honor.

Q: *What is the difference between a catfish and a lawyer.*
A: One is a bottom-dwelling, garbage-eating scavenger. The other is a fish.

Q: *What is the difference between a lawyer and a rooster?*
A: The rooster clucks defiance.

PRACTICING LAW

reason 27. HEEDING THE LAW SIREN'S SONG

*I dreamed that as a lawyer I would be a sort of Warrior/
Artist who fought for clients, but fought for Justice above all.
Instead, I found myself in a sort of ethical cave where
attorneys function as shadowy clerks spending their time
copying documents requested by their clients with little regard
to concepts of fairness and right. And perhaps even more
sadly, I discovered that the attorneys themselves were all
fungible, as interchangeable as their copying machines.*

F. Hayden Curry
University of Virginia School of Law
Occupation: Artist and Builder

Tie yourself to the mast. Stuff your ears with bubble gum. Cover your eyes with rounds of bologna. There is a seductress loose in the land who tempts the idealistic and attracts those who seek after Truth and Justice. Her song is simple: wrongs can be righted, causes can be launched and a new, more beautiful world forged by idealistic lawyers.

Reality is different. Law has tarried so long in the pockets of the Powers That Be that it has become the essential ingredient in the glue that binds us to the status quo.

Viewed from a distance, The Law Siren shimmers with many bright guises—all implying that anything is possible through the study and application of the law. The Siren is an expert at mirroring your own desire and will tell you exactly what you want to hear—that law can be used to create a new environmental order, to end all war, to desegregate schools, to protect the rights of the indigent, or whatever else is important to you. Viewed up close, this is not the case. But if you are close enough to The Law Siren to discover this, it will already be too late. You will be a lawyer.

The Law Siren is dangerous precisely because she tells you that, through the law, you can fight for your beliefs in a way that will fulfill your most idealistic view of yourself, but still give you enough spare change to buy designer sunglasses. The hard truth is that the hungry need food, the homeless need shelter, and all the world needs peace. But no one needs more lawyers. If the 900,000 or so lawyers already minted are not up to solving our problems, it's unlikely that you will help much.

But what, you ask, about all the good and noble legal victories won by the Clarence Darrows of our legal tradition? Get bigger pieces of Double Bubble for your ears; some of The Law Siren's music is obviously getting through. To counter it, consider a few areas where lawyers have honestly and zealously dedicated themselves to reforming the world by court order.

• **Education:** *Brown v. Board of Education* ordered the desegregation of schools in 1954. Today, the schools are more segregated than ever. If racial balance improves in the future, it will be because people have learned to live with one another, not because a judge ordered it.

• **Environment:** Major environmental lawsuits have been with us for at least two decades. Despite a few isolated victories, the forces that would abuse the air, water and land have hardly been slowed by the wave of the judicial wand. The water and air may clear eventually, but not because environmental lawyers helped with the cleaning.

• **Poverty:** The first generation of bright, committed, hardworking Legal Aid lawyers became disillusioned and quit when they realized that every time they won a court victory guaranteeing one group of low-income people more money, the government simply cut back another equally deserving program. Despite political about-faces and many pronouncements about the essentialness of pro bono lawyering to help the indigent, the tide has yet to turn.

• **Criminal Procedure:** *Gideon v. Wainwright* established that a low-income person charged with any crime has the right to a lawyer. The result has been that many thousands more public defenders, district attorneys and judges live off the public purse at great cost to the taxpayer. Nearly the same percentage of low income defendants end up in jail as before they all had legal assistance.

reason 28. KEEPING HOLY THE FEES

A number of years ago, one of the partners circulated an advertisement for a book published by Prentice-Hall on how to make more money practicing law. It stated:

"To the attorney who wants something more than the $50,000 [it would be $150,000 today] a year most attorneys call success... Stop wasting time on unprofitable cases ... it takes courage to drop clients, even though they're not as profitable as they should be. But you're not going to build your practice or make your fortune without courage."

Recognizing my cowardly nature, I resigned.

ANONYMOUS
Harvard University Law School
Occupation: Librarian

The Scene

A state Senate hearing to consider proposed legislation to make it easier for non-lawyers to represent themselves in divorce proceedings. Although the public hearing was announced a month in advance, the time and place changed six times. The hearing finally convenes in an unmarked storage area in the Capitol basement.

Those Present

Twelve members of the State Senate Judiciary Committee—all lawyers.

Six legislative assistants—four lawyers, two recent law school graduates studying for the Bar Exam at night.

Four representatives of various state agencies, including the Judicial Council, Administrator of the State Courts, the Attorney General's office and Office of Professional Standards—all lawyers.

Five representatives of interested private groups who wish to present testimony and just happened to be told of the room

change, including the State Bar Association, the United Trial Lawyers, the Domestic Litigation Committee, the Association of Court Conciliators, and the Trial Judges Committee—all lawyers.

Two committee secretaries—one in night law school and one married to a lawyer.

One member of the public, Abner Cristo—a janitor in state employ mopping behind a pile of discarded furniture in the corner. Abner is not a lawyer, although he took a law school correspondence course for six months. Unfortunately, he lost the matchbook containing the school's address and couldn't continue. Despite all that, he regularly says "pursuant" and "moreover" and brings his two sandwiches and small bottle of muscatel to work in a gold-initialed briefcase.

THOSE ABSENT

Representatives of several consumer organizations and Nolo Press, publisher of self-help law books—one lawyer, several dropped-out lawyers and an earnest former paralegal—who, as a result of an accidental oversight by the committee secretary in night law school, were not notified of the room change. All are lost at various locations in the Capitol.

OPENING REMARKS BY THE CHAIRPERSON OF THE JUDICIARY COMMITTEE

"It has been brought to our attention that if we enact Senate Bill 312, the divorce law of this state can be easily simplified so that any fool who can get a driver's license can do his or her own divorce without the need for a lawyer."

CLOSING REMARKS BY THE CHAIRPERSON OF THE JUDICIARY COMMITTEE (AFTER TWO HOURS OF TESTIMONY)

"It seems absolutely clear to me, after listening to the enlightened testimony of the members of the general public, that there is no public sentiment in favor of simplifying divorce procedures, and that so doing might even cause economic hardship and unemployment to a certain deserving group of citizens. Let's table the divorce reform bill for this year, recess for lunch and then consider the Bar Association's proposal that all civil trials be conducted in Latin."

reason 29. HATING YOUR CLIENTS

You ask why I quit the practice of law?

*I hate conflict. Besides, what do I care about some stranger,
let alone his problems?*

> DENIS CLIFFORD
> Columbia University School of Law
> Occupation: Author and Soldier of Fortune

Imagine that you have successfully graduated from law school. Those fellow and fellowette students you learned to loathe—The Drudge, The Compulsive Talker, The Paranoid and The Ass Kisser—are now your professional colleagues at the Bar.

Now come the clients—large, small, civil, criminal, plaintiff, defendant, incarcerated, inebriated, lacerated and so on. They have only one thing in common: a problem—one so miserably impossible to resolve that they are willing to pay you upwards of $200 an hour to try.

Probate and Estate Planning Clients: Have typically just lost a loved one and are usually feeling bereft, depressed, guilty, bitter, worried, vengeful or all of the aforelisted. In addition, they have all heard what a rip-off the probate process is and are fully prepared to hate you no matter how well you perform. Because in your heart you know you are charging far too much to handle a procedure that should have been eliminated 50 years ago, you will feel guilty enough to accept the blame.

Domestic Clients: Are normally involved in a divorce, child custody, alimony, palimony or paternity dispute. They tend to be hostile, depressed, guilty, bitter, worried, vengeful and armed to the teeth—usually all seven.

Personal Injury Clients—Legitimate: Most of these are in physical pain as well as depressed, worried, bitter and vengeful. They are delighted that you will take their cases for no money down and a percentage of the recovery until you win and they realize that after costs for four depositions, six expert witnesses and their sky-high medical bills have been subtracted from their share, you somehow wound up with a hefty five-figure fee and they got $281. At this point, they all decide you are a schmuck. A few arm themselves to the teeth.

Personal Injury Clients—Phony: The good thing about these people is that they are not in physical pain, depressed, worried, bitter or vengeful. They are merely greedy. There are two other bad things about them.

1. They have cynically manufactured a fraudulent whiplash, twisted back or esoteric phobia.

2. From long experience, they have learned how to prevent you from ending up with most of any settlement.

You ought to toss them out of your office. Perhaps you will, but when faced with trying to make a living in a world where traffic accidents are falling almost as fast as lawyers are increasing, you might be tempted to join the 33.3% of lawyers that studies have shown are willing to counsel clients on phony personal injury claims.

Immigration Clients: This is one area where there is no dearth of potential clients. At last count, nearly two billion non-Americans were seeking a good immigration lawyer to get them

or keep them in the United States. This may present no problem for you if you want to arrange quasi-legal business visas, quasi-fraudulent marriages and look the other way when yet another person who speaks a remote Serbo-Croatian dialect appears in your waiting room with a birth certificate verifying that he was born in Okema, Oklahoma.

Business Clients: As a rule, these people are happier and richer than most other clients. They are nice to their spouses, good to their children and give to the United Way. They reserve their hostility for their business competitors, whom they would dearly love to draw, quarter and assault with plastique if it wouldn't put their membership on the Symphony Board at risk. Instead, when angry, they take long deep breaths, pick up their cellular phones and call their agent provocateurs in charge of dispensing hostility. That would be you. Putting unpleasantness behind them, they happily tee up for the 7th hole, remarking that they just tossed a piece of red meat to the company shark.

reason 30. BECOMING A SOLE PRACTITIONER

During a court appearance, I was sketching a dozing judge. My client looked over my shoulder and said: "You ought to be an artist." And it wasn't long before I agreed that he was right. It's been over 30 years that I've been drawing things other than bills of complaint.

WYNN KAPITZ
University of Miami School of Law
Occupation: Designer, *The Anatomy Coloring Book*

If you decide to open your own law practice, the first thing you have to do is teach yourself the law. The hatful of theories you may have picked up in law school is piteously insufficient ammunition with which to file the simplest pleading at your local courthouse.

Before you can acquire the requisite experience, you need to find your first guinea pig—aka client—who is willing to subsidize this phase of your legal education.

To attract clients, you will need to find an office over which to hang your shingle. This is increasingly hard to do. After all, what clear thinking landlord would rent to a lawyer? And assuming you're lucky enough to find space, you will still need to hire at least some staff to fill it. These days, it's difficult to find a paralegal or legal secretary who isn't belligerently mutinous. With good reason. If they're competent in the least, they already know more about the day-to-day practice of law than you do. If you bring a lot of work for them to do they will be justifiably upset because, despite your ignorance, you pay yourself far more than you pay them. And if you don't find any clients, they will be even more upset because you won't be able to pay them at all.

Which brings the circle around to the dilemma of finding that first client. Given the current dog-eat-dog nature of the profession, you, as a neophyte with neither skills nor experience, will probably be reduced to placing ads.

Headache? Cough? Feeling blue? Somewhere, someone with insurance can be made to pay! Let me find the deep pocket that's tailor-made for you. Eager lawyer seeks anyone with the slightest injury. It's the 90s. Sue or be sued.

or

Lonely lawyer looking for seriously injured male/female for lasting, lucrative relationship. I see us together for years, going to pre-trial conferences, hearings, trial and appeals. Together we'll shake down whoever injured you and live happily ever after on the settlement. I'm a sensitive guy. Juries love me. You will too.

No matter how you slice it, street corner law is a tacky business.

LAWYERS BEREFT OF SERVICE — WHO IN HER RIGHT MIND WOULD WORK FOR, RENT TO, OR MINISTER TO A LAWYER?

reason 31. CHOOSING A SPECIALTY

My first and only job as a lawyer was with a personal injury firm. Ninety-five percent of our cases involved car crashes and ninety-five percent of those were settled without a trial. So, I spent my days on the phone negotiating with insurance adjusters. Basically, I was using the law to blackmail insurance companies into doing what they should have done in the first place. I soon found something better to do. I sailed a yacht to Tahiti.

WILLIAM RODARMOR
Columbia University School of Law
Occupation: Magazine Editor

No one believes in generalists anymore. In medicine, internists have been replaced by a host of Allergists and Immunologists, Endogrinologists, Neurologists, Gastroenterologists and various other extremely specialized Ologists. If you want to be a successful lawyer—that is, one who inspires confusion and awe in all around them—you will almost surely have to specialize in some area of law.

The P.I. Law Firm Ordinaire: Imagine yourself hanging around the watercooler with people who are actively rooting for someone who has suffered a serious misfortune to walk, or better yet, wheel through your firm's door. You know you are about to make Partner when you find yourself rubbing your hands at the thought of a new quadriplegic client.

The P.I. Law Firm Extraordinaire—Airline crashes, chemical spills, nuclear disasters and other large catastrophes: As a new lawyer, your main job will be to fly to obscure disaster locations, open a temporary office and attend numerous funerals. Here you will find yourself lined three deep with other disaster lawyers, tossing your card at the victim's family. (To develop the necessary wrist motions, law firm associates spend hours scaling baseball cards into the umbrella stand.) With the internationalization of tort law, if you can say: "I can get you big bucks" in forty or more languages, you are almost sure to be a success.

The Criminal Law Firm: Imagine joining forces with that cadre of armed and mostly inebriated lawyers who regularly defend the nation's criminals.

- All of your clients will be guilty and many will secretly scare you silly.

- As a result, you will lose most trials. This is depressing in and of itself.

- As a result, you will find yourself on the shit lists of a large number of hostile, revenge-consumed, homicidal types who will eventually be walking the same streets you are. This is even more depressing.

- As a result, you will buy one or more guns which you will stash here and there around your living and working quarters. This will be scary to your spouse and kids and

AMERICAN LAWYERS BEGAN JETTING AROUND THE WORLD ON THE HEELS OF EVERY MAJOR DISASTER — IN THE 1990's, SEVERAL AGGRESSIVE LAWFIRMS GOT THERE FIRST.

they will begin to regard you in the same light as they do your clients. Most depressing.

Sports Law: This one sounds glamorous. The goal is to find a few athletes with six million dollar salaries and take 10% for negotiating a new contract now and then. The reality is that to do that, you have to sign up a small herd of junior high school athletes and more or less support the ungrateful, sex-crazed, substance-abusers for the next decade. And even if you manage to do this without going nuts, the very few really good ones are likely to:

- injure some part of themselves you've never heard of

- get bought off by another lawyer

- drive their first Porsche into a goalpost after snorting something commonly used to tranquilize turkeys, or

- all of the above.

reason 32. MAKING RAIN

I arrived at my first job at a public interest law firm shaking with excitement—all hyped to dig into the firm's work, which was to provide legal assistance to low-income clients. My supervising's attorney's first words to me were: Do you have a tuxedo yet?

Anonymous
Georgetown University Law Center
Occupation: Aerobics Instructor and Soup Kitchen
Coordinator

As a lawyer, you will not be regarded as an asset to a firm—and will have few assets yourself—unless you perfect the art of

POLO... SQUASH... TENNIS ANYONE?

ingratiating yourself. In legal parlance, this is known as Being a Rainmaker. In real life, the quaint coinage translates to shaking hands and shaking down bucks.

All the firm loves a Rainmaker because they do things everyone else finds too distasteful, including:

• Attending local, state and national bar association meetings—events at which lawyers give lectures to rooms full of other lawyers, after which they meet casually and try to impress one another with the details of their most recent big case.

• Attending Continuing Education of the Bar classes—events at which lawyers give lectures to rooms full of other lawyers, after which they meet casually and try to impress one another with the details of their most recent big case.

• Attending cocktail parties at other lawyers' houses—events at which lawyers give lectures to rooms full of other lawyers, after which they meet casually and try to impress one another with the details of their most recent big case.

reason 33. PRACTICING LEGAL ETHICS

Legal Ethics comes down to one word: money. Fairness, kindness, a commitment to helping people resolve their own disputes are all irrelevant. When I realized that even my best friend had an ethical duty to screw me if that's where the money was, I quit practicing law.

BARBARA MOULTON
GEORGE WASHINGTON UNIVERSITY NATIONAL LAW CENTER
OCCUPATION: SMALL CLAIMS ADVISOR

Like Military Intelligence, Legal Ethics is often jokingly described as an oxymoron. What do you make of a profession in which thousands of consumer complaints are swept under the rug, it can take up to five years to disbar the worst crook and no testing or peer review is ever done to see if members remain competent?

And consider Frequent Flier Miles—the euphemism routinely used to describe kick-backs paid to lawyers who schedule extra-long depositions.

It works like this:

Lawyers are given premiums by court reporter services in many states based on the length of depositions; the more pages of testimony, the better prizes. Thus, a lawyer who simply refrains from asking a garrulous witness to get to the point, not only ups billable hours, but also earns nifty gifts.

Many court reporting outfits offer lawyers catalogs from which to choose gift certificates for items. Popular items include massages, car detailing, champagne brunches, hypnotherapy and skin rejuvenation.

Legal Ethics doesn't extend to fessing up that in addition to paying you $250 an hour, your client just treated your Mercedes to a reconditioning.

The clients who end up paying for all this never complain about it.

They aren't told.

reason 34. PRACTICING CREATIVE ACCOUNTING

I spent a fascinating four years as a small cog in a large law machine. There, all young associates—often called "profit centers"—were supposed to produce enough income to exceed their cost to the firm by a substantial amount. This was necessary to compensate for those senior partners for which the reverse was true.

DOUG CARLSTON
Harvard University Law School
Occupation: President, Software Company

If you enter practice with a private firm, you will quickly be taught how to keep two sets of books—one for your clients, the other for your boss. And then, as a matter of personal sanity and survival, you'll need to keep a third set for yourself. The idea, of course, is that the firm will want to bill your clients for a highly exaggerated number of hours, while paying you for as few as possible.

Unit Billing: This billing system requires a unique lawyer's clock which contains no division smaller than the quarter hour. Truly advanced firms only use half hour clocks. It works like this: No matter what portion of a quarter hour is spent on a particular client's business, you will compute your billing time to the next quarter hour. Thus, if you talk to a client for three minutes on the phone, you bill for 15 minutes. If the call lasts 16 minutes, you bill for a half hour, and so on.

Billing Lawyer Rates for Secretary Time: Most legal jobs involve a hefty amount of repetitive paper shuffling and form preparation which could be accomplished by a chimpanzee. Your firm, which will grudgingly pay you $50,000 per year ($25 per hour) while it bills your clients $200 per hour for your time,

will expect you to unload as much work as possible on your secretary or paralegal, who gets paid $12 per hour.

Efficiency Billing: This is the current rage at large law firms. You compute how long it takes you to accomplish a legal task the first time you do it. Say that the first spousal trust you tackle takes three hours. Ten trusts later, you are able to accomplish the same task in 17 minutes. Bill your client for the entire three hours. This is extremely efficient. For the firm.

reason 35. MAKING PARTNER

*My enjoyment of practicing law with a good-sized firm was
hampered by three factors. I didn't like the work. I didn't like
the other lawyers. And I didn't like the clients. Nothing I've
done in the years since I quit the law has been nearly as
boring.*

ROBERT FLAHERTY
University of Michigan Law School
Occupation: Restaurateur

Everyone who reads a novel featuring a successful lawyer knows
all about the rewards that come with partnership in a top-drawer
firm—the $600,000 draw (in a bad year), membership in a spiffy

country club, March in the Virgin Islands. Unfortunately, while being a senior partner isn't too hard to take—except for your colleagues—the road to senior partnershiphood is not an easy one to tread.

Hint 1: Start Early. Plan to be born white, male and Protestant. If you can't manage this, try female, black, Buddhist and handicapped—it's hard for even the stuffiest firm to resist a quadruple minority if, in addition, she is also the editor of the Harvard Law Review and agrees not to complain about being excluded from the country club. (See Hint 2, below.)

Hint 2: Build Character. From the get-go, not only must you pile your blocks higher than any of the other kids, you must also learn to kick over the piles of the other smart kids' blocks without getting caught. Later this will be called Aggressive Advocacy and praised to the hilt. Your only goal in your school years is to be number one in everything so that you are sure to be accepted at Yale, Harvard, or Princeton. Four other schools will also work. If you have to ask which ones, you'd be better off setting your sights on the legal department of a mid-sized insurance company in the Midwest.

Hint 3: Think of Little Else. When you reach Yale, you must study maniacally so that you graduate with honors, score at least 750 on your law boards, and get accepted at Harvard Law School. There are eight, maybe ten, other law schools that will keep at least one foot on the partnership ladder and several hundred others that won't.

Hint 4: Work on Law Review. Not only must you study 20 hours a day, so as to place in the top 10% of all your desperately over-achieving classmates and be selected for the law review— the real one, not *Legal Ecotactics* or *The Environmental Protection Quarterly*. And your law review contribution must demonstrate that your views are sound. Say a kind word about feudalism. Or if you want to be daringly modern, praise the Supreme Court under the leadership of William Howard Taft.

Hint 5: Dress for Repress. This is critical. More than one law review editor has blown it all at that ever-important employ-ment interview by wearing a blue shirt instead of a white one. Men should wear ties covered with small pheasants. Mallards in flight are acceptable, but crossed golf clubs almost guarantee that you will end up working for a small firm in the suburbs. Women at all costs must avoid Gucci, Pucci, or even Yves Saint Laurent and instead wear sensible tweeds in the style favored by the English royal family in 1938.

If you have successfully followed hints one through five, you should now be an associate at an acceptable firm. But the ladder will still stretch far above you—and each ascending rung will be more slippery than the one below. You must realize that, increasingly, most associates can't make it all the way to full partner but are let go when their youthful fire and energy begin to ebb.

Hint 6: Be There. Stay at work until nine in the evening. And be sure to show up first on Saturday and Sunday mornings. In the more liberal big firms, it is permissible to wear a blue shirt on the weekends.

Hint 7: Make the Most—or Least—of the Past. If you went to Princeton, Amherst or Stanford (West Coast only), have your alumni magazine delivered to your office. If you went to college at Cornell or Michigan, or even worse, a state college, it's best to have all annoying reminders of your alma mater sent to your home.

Hint 8: Frequent the Right Court. If you play racquetball, quickly change to squash. If you play tennis, be sure you use a wooden racquet. If you play polo, place a small picture of your horse in a modest silver frame on the corner of your desk.

Hint 9: Order Lunch in French. Of course, you know French. If you don't, you will probably want to resign quietly—although you may be able to slide by for a while by announcing that as long as the Frogs vote Socialist, you will never eat another bite of cassoulet (kass-oo-lay).

Hint 10: Save Your Money. Your starting salary will be about $60,000 and, of course, you'll get generous raises. Unfortunately, it won't last. Big firms are never so crude as to fire anyone. But when your cubicle is reduced to a broom closet, your secretary mysteriously disappears, and you haven't had Oysters Rockefeller and Pommes Frites with a partner since you had that trouble with the Collingworth bonds, you will realize that, at age 35, you are on your way out. In addition, you have a bad stomach, high child support payments, an over-developed taste for Wild Turkey, tendonitis (from all that squash), and, almost without noticing it, you have been transformed from Up and Coming to Down and Going.

Not only that, you have little experience and few legal skills which are valuable outside the world of Big Firms, and therefore, you are probably unemployable as a lawyer. No Big Firm will ever hire anyone eased out by another Big Firm. Your best bet is to apply for a teaching job at a law school—the only places interested in credentials that add up to little or nothing.

reason 36. YOU MIGHT GET TO BE A JUDGE

Aside from the biblical warning that it is almost sure to come back to haunt you, there are several more practical reasons why donning the robe is a downer.

• You will have to listen to all those attorneys you used to avoid at cocktail parties.

• The robes itch.

• None of your friends will share a joint with you

> DOUG HILL
> University of California at Berkeley School of Law
> Occupation: Business Person

Witness a page from the new book, Pontificating From Above—
A Student's Guide to Jobs in the Field of Shouting Down at
People From Platforms. Skip past the sections on Ministers,
Circus Barkers, Tennis Referees and College Lecturers and turn
directly to Judges. It reads:

While it's true that law school is a bore, studying for the bar
exam miserable and practicing law unbelievably petty and full of
tacky little details, it will all be worthwhile if you have the
foresight to make friends with the right politician and are
appointed to the bench. Among the principal advantages of
being a judge are:

• You get to spend up to eight hours a day looking out at the
world from a really splendid, elevated throne.

• You get to dress in a handsome black nightgown, appropri-
ately funereal, which scares many of the people who talk to you.
See our English edition for information about those curly white
wigs that have sadly been eliminated in the colonies.

• You get your own dandy little hammer which you are free to
bang briskly whenever anyone is the least bit impolite.

A Day in the Fantasy Life of a Judge

• Your former law school classmates, even the haughtiest ones, must stand when you ascend your throne. Even better, they must call you "Your Honor," and, if they are really anxious that you do something, say "Pray the Court" or "May it please the Court." Unfortunately, kneeling and bowing have been eliminated.

• And best of all, if anyone speaks to you roughly or is disrespectful of your authority, you get to exorcise your accumulated frustrations by nodding down to your armed bailiff—a comfortably big former junior college football player who does his best to keep the local brewery solvent—who will grab the bothersome soul and escort him or her to the nearest steel cage. This almost always has a salutary effect on the other people who come before you who are now much more willing to conduct themselves in a properly obsequious manner.

ABOUT THE AUTHORS

Ralph Warner, Boalt Hall School of Law, University of California, is currently a writer and publisher.

Toni Ihara, King Hall School of Law, University of California, is currently a graphic designer and writer.

Barbara Kate Repa, currently a writer and editor, graduated from law school a while back and remembers very little about the experience.

ABOUT THE ARTIST

Mari Stein, who never quite completed her law school application, is currently an artist, writer and yoga teacher.

Just for Fun

Poetic Justice

The funniest, Meanest things ever said about lawyers. . .

Edited by Jonathan and Andrew Roth

An exuberant collection of thoughts about the legal profession by poets and writers of every culture and century.

$9.95/PJ

Nolo's Favorite Lawyer Jokes

Over 200 jokes and hilariously nasty remarks about lawyers. 100% guaranteed to produce an evening of chuckles, spice up an after-dinner speech and drive your lawyer relatives nuts.

Macintosh $9.95/JODM
Windows $9.95/JODWI

NOLO PRESS
25 YEARS
LAW FOR ALL

CATALOG
...more from Nolo Press

	EDITION	PRICE	CODE

	EDITION	PRICE	CODE
Business Plans to Game Plans	1st	$29.95	GAME
Getting Started as an Independent Paralegal—Audio	2nd	$44.95	GSIP
Helping Employees Achieve Retirement Security	1st	$16.95	HEAR
How to Finance a Growing Business	4th	$24.95	GROW
How to Form a CA Nonprofit Corp.—w/Corp. Records Binder & PC Disk	1st	$49.95	CNP
How to Form a Nonprofit Corp., Book w/Disk (PC)—National Edition	2nd	$39.95	NNP
How to Form Your Own Calif. Corp.—w/Corp. Records Binder & Disk—PC	1st	$39.95	CACI
How to Form Your Own California Corporation	8th	$29.95	CCOR
How to Form Your Own Florida Corporation, (Book w/Disk—PC)	3rd	$39.95	FLCO
How to Form Your Own New York Corporation, (Book w/Disk—PC)	3rd	$39.95	NYCO
How to Form Your Own Texas Corporation, (Book w/Disk—PC)	4th	$39.95	TCI
How to Market a Product for Under $500	1st	$29.95	UN500

	EDITION	PRICE	CODE

CONSUMER

	EDITION	PRICE	CODE
Fed Up With the Legal System: What's Wrong & How to Fix It	2nd	$9.95	LEG
Glossary of Insurance Terms	5th	$14.95	GLINT
How to Insure Your Car	1st	$12.95	INCAR
How to Win Your Personal Injury Claim	1st	$24.95	PICL
Nolo's Law Form Kit: Hiring Child Care & Household Help	1st	$14.95	KCHLD
Nolo's Pocket Guide to California Law	3rd	$10.95	CLAW
Nolo's Pocket Guide to California Law on Disk—Windows	3.0	$17.46	CLW3
Nolo's Pocket Guide to Consumer Rights (California Edition)	2nd	$12.95	CAG
Nolo's Pocket Guide to Consumer Rights (California Edition)	2nd	$12.95	CAG
The Over 50 Insurance Survival Guide	1st	$16.95	OVER50
True Odds: How Risk Affects Your Everyday Life	1st	$19.95	TROD
What Do You Mean It's Not Covered?	1st	$19.95	COVER

ESTATE PLANNING & PROBATE

	EDITION	PRICE	CODE
5 Ways to Avoid Probate—Audio	1st	$14.95	TPRO
How to Probate an Estate (California Edition)	8th	$34.95	PAE
Make Your Own Living Trust	1st	$19.95	LITR
Nolo's Law Form Kit: Wills	1st	$14.95	KWL
Nolo's Simple Will Book	2nd	$17.95	SWIL
Plan Your Estate	3rd	$24.95	NEST

TO ORDER CALL 800-992-6656

	EDITION	PRICE	CODE
How to Write a Business Plan	4th	$21.95	SBS
Make Up Your Mind: Entrepreneurs Talk About Decision Making	1st	$19.95	MIND
Managing Generation X: How to Bring Out the Best in Young Talent	1st	$19.95	MANX
Marketing Without Advertising	1st	$14.00	MWAD
Mastering Diversity: Managing for Success Under ADA and Other Anti-Discrimination Laws	1st	$29.95	MAST
OSHA in the Real World:(Book w/ Disk—PC)	1st	$29.95	OSHA
Small Business Legal Pro—Macintosh	2nd	$25.97	SBM2
Small Business Legal Pro—Windows	2nd	$25.97	SBWI2
Taking Care of Your Corporation, Vol. 1, (Book w/Disk—PC)	1st	$26.95	CORK
Taking Care of Your Corporation, Vol 2, (Book w/Disk—PC)	1st	$39.95	CORK2
Tax Savvy for Small Business	1st	$26.95	SAVVY
The California Nonprofit Corporation Handbook	7th	$29.95	NON
The California Professional Corporation Handbook	5th	$34.95	PROF
The Employer's Legal Handbook	1st	$29.95	EMPL
The Independent Paralegal's Handbook	3rd	$29.95	PARA
The Legal Guide for Starting & Running a Small Business	2nd	$24.95	RUNS
The Partnership Book: How to Write a Partnership Agreement	4th	$24.95	PART
Trademark: How to Name Your Business & Product	2nd	$29.95	TRD

TO ORDER CALL 800-992-6656

	EDITION	PRICE	CODE
The Quick and Legal Will Book	1st	$15.95	QUIC
Write Your Will—Audio	1st	$14.95	TWYW

FAMILY MATTERS

	EDITION	PRICE	CODE
A Legal Guide for Lesbian and Gay Couples	8th	$24.95	LG
Child Custody: Building Agreements That Work	1st	$24.95	CUST
Divorce & Money: How to Make the Best Financial Decisions During Divorce	2nd	$21.95	DIMO
How to Adopt Your Stepchild in California	4th	$22.95	ADOP
How to Do Your Own Divorce in California	20th	$21.95	CDIV
How to Do Your Own Divorce in Texas	5th	$17.95	TDIV
How to Raise or Lower Child Support in California	3rd	$18.95	CHLD
Nolo's Pocket Guide to Family Law	3rd	$14.95	FLD
Practical Divorce Solutions	1st	$14.95	PDS
The Guardianship Book (California Edition)	2nd	$24.95	GB
The Living Together Kit	7th	$24.95	LTK

GOING TO COURT

	EDITION	PRICE	CODE
Collect Your Court Judgment (California Edition)	2nd	$19.95	JUDG
Everybody's Guide to Municipal Court (California Edition)	1st	$29.95	MUNI
Everybody's Guide to Small Claims Court (California Edition)	11th	$18.95	CSCC
Everybody's Guide to Small Claims Court (National Edition)	6th	$18.95	NSCC
Fight Your Ticket ... and Win! (California Edition)	6th	$19.95	FYT

TO ORDER CALL 800-992-6656

	EDITION	PRICE	CODE
How to Change Your Name (California Edition)	6th	$24.95	NAME
Represent Yourself in Court: How to Prepare & Try a Winning Case........................	1st	$29.95	RYC
The Criminal Records Book (California Edition)..	4th	$21.95	CRIM
Winning in Small Claims Court—Audio..	1st	$14.95	TWIN

HOMEOWNERS, LANDLORDS & TENANTS

Dog Law..	2nd	$12.95	DOG
Every Landlord's Legal Guide (Book w/ Disk—PC).......................................	1st	$29.95	ELLI
For Sale by Owner (California Edition)	2nd	$24.95	FSBO
Homestead Your House (California Edition)	8th	$9.95	HOME
How to Buy a House in California..	3rd	$24.95	BHCA
Neighbor Law: Fences, Trees, Boundaries & Noise	2nd	$16.95	NEI
Nolo's Law Form Kit: Leases & Rental Agreements (California Edition)......................	1st	$14.95	KLEAS
Safe Homes, Safe Neighborhoods: Stopping Crime Where You Live	1st	$14.95	SAFE
Tenants' Rights (California Edition)	12th	$18.95	CTEN
The Deeds Book (California Edition)..	3rd	$16.95	DEED
The Landlord's Law Book, Vol. 1: Rights & Responsibilities (California Edition)	4th	$32.95	LBRT
The Landlord's Law Book, Vol. 2: Evictions (California Edition).............................	5th	$34.95	LBEV

HUMOR

29 Reasons Not to Go to Law School	4th	$9.95	29R
Nolo's Favorite Lawyer Jokes On Disk—DOS...	1.0	$9.95	JODI

	EDITION	PRICE	CODE
Stand Up to the IRS	2nd	$21.95	SIRS

PATENTS AND COPYRIGHTS

	EDITION	PRICE	CODE
Copyright Your Software	1st	$39.95	CYS
Patent, Copyright & Trademark: A Desk Reference to Intellectual Property Law	1ST	$24.95	PCTM
Patent It Yourself	4th	$39.95	PAT
Software Development: A Legal Guide (Book with disk—PC)	1st	$44.95	SFT
The Copyright Handbook: How to Protect and Use Written Works	2nd	$24.95	COHA
The Inventor's Notebook	1st	$19.95	INOT

RESEARCH & REFERENCE

	EDITION	PRICE	CODE
Law on the Net	1st	$39.95	LAWN
Legal Research: How to Find & Understand the Law	4th	$19.95	LRES
Legal Research Made Easy: A Roadmap through the Law Library Maze—Video	1st	$89.95	LRME

SENIORS

	EDITION	PRICE	CODE
Beat the Nursing Home Trap: A Consumer's Guide	2nd	$18.95	ELD
Social Security, Medicare & Pensions	6th	$19.95	SOA
The Conservatorship Book (California Edition)	2nd	$29.95	CNSV

SOFTWARE

	EDITION	PRICE	CODE
California Incorporator 1.0—DOS	1.0	$47.97	INCI
Living Trust Maker 2.0—Macintosh	2.0	$47.97	LTM2

TO ORDER CALL 800-992-6656

	EDITION	PRICE	CODE
Nolo's Favorite Lawyer Jokes On Disk—Macintosh	1.0	$9.95	JODM
Nolo's Favorite Lawyer Jokes On Disk—Windows	1st	$9.95	JODWI
Poetic Justice: The Funniest, Meanest Things Ever Said About Lawyers	1st	$9.95	PJ

IMMIGRATION

	EDITION	PRICE	CODE
Como Obtener La Tarjeta Verde: Maneras Legitimas de Permanecer en los EE.UU.	1st	$24.95	VERDE
How to Become a United States Citizen	5th	$14.95	CIT
How to Get a Green Card: Legal Ways to Stay in the U.S.A.	2nd	$24.95	GRN
U.S. Immigration Made Easy	5th	$39.95	IMEZ

MONEY MATTERS

	EDITION	PRICE	CODE
Building Your Nest Egg With Your 401(k)	1st	$16.95	EGG
Chapter 13 Bankruptcy: Repay Your Debts	1st	$29.95	CHI3
How to File for Bankruptcy	5th	$25.95	HFB
Money Troubles: Legal Strategies to Cope With Your Debts	3rd	$18.95	MT
Nolo's Law Form Kit: Buy & Sell Contracts	1st	$9.95	KCONT
Nolo's Law Form Kit: Personal Bankruptcy	1st	$14.95	KBNK
Nolo's Law Form Kit: Personal Loan Agreements for Friends & Family	1st	$14.95	KLOAN
Nolo's Law Form Kit: Power of Attorney	1st	$14.95	KPA
Nolo's Law Form Kit: Rebuild Your Credit	1st	$14.95	KCRD
Simple Contracts for Personal Use	2nd	$16.95	CONT
Smart Ways to Save Money During and After Divorce	1st	$14.95	SAVMO

	EDITION	PRICE	CODE
Living Trust Maker 2.0—Windows	2.0	$47.97	LTWI2
Nolo's Partnership Maker 1.0—DOS	1.0	$47.97	PAGI1
Nolo's Personal RecordKeeper 3.0—Macintosh	3.0	$29.97	FRM3
Patent It Yourself 1.0—Windows	1.0	$149.47	PYW1
WillMaker 5.0—DOS	5.0	$48.96	WI5
WillMaker 5.0—Macintosh	5.0	$41.97	WM5
WillMaker 6.0—Windows	6.0	$41.97	WIW6

WORKPLACE

	EDITION	PRICE	CODE
How to Handle Your Workers' Compensation Claim (California Edition)	1st	$29.95	WORK
Rightful Termination	1st	$29.95	RITE
Sexual Harassment on the Job	2nd	$18.95	HARS
Workers' Comp for Employers	2nd	$29.95	CNTRL
Your Rights in the Workplace	2nd	$15.95	YRW

SPECIAL UPGRADE OFFER

GET 25% OFF THE LATEST EDITION OF YOUR NOLO BOOK

It's important to have the most current legal information. Because laws and legal procedures change often, we update our books regularly. To help keep you up-to-date we are extending this special upgrade offer. Cut out and mail the title portion of the cover of your old Nolo book and we'll give you 25% off the retail price of the NEW EDITION when you purchase directly from us. For more information call us at 1-800-992-6656. This offer is to individuals only.

TO ORDER CALL 800-992-6656

ORDER FORM

Code	Quantity	Title	Unit price	Total

Subtotal	
In California add Appropriate Sales Tax	
Shipping & Handling: $5 for 1 item; $6 for 2-3 items $7 for 4 or more.	
UPS RUSH delivery $7-any size order•	
TOTAL	

Name

Address

UPS to street address, Priority Mail to P.O. boxes.   S.F. Bay area & P.O. Box use regular shipping

• Delivered in 3 business days from receipt of order

FOR FASTER SERVICE, USE YOUR CREDIT CARD AND OUR TOLL-FREE NUMBERS

Order 24 hours a day	1 (800) 992-6656
General Information	1 (510) 549-1976
Fax your order	1 (800) 645-0895
e-mail	Noloinfo@nolopress.com
Customer service	1-800-728-3555, Mon.-Sat. 9am-5pm, PST

OR mail us your order with a check or money order made payable to:

Nolo Press, 950 Parker St., Berkeley, CA 94710

METHOD OF PAYMENT

☐ Check enclosed

☐ VISA   ☐ MasterCard   ☐ Discover Card   ☐ American Express

Account #   Expiration Date

Authorizing Signature

Daytime Phone

VISIT OUR STORE

If you live in the Bay Area, be sure to visit the Nolo Press Bookstore on the corner of 9th and Parker Streets in west Berkeley. You'll find our complete line of books and software—all at a discount. Call 1-510-704-2248 for hours.

PRICES SUBJECT TO CHANGE   PJ 4.2